Angela Newland lives in Essex with her family and three dogs. She has worked as an administrator for many years and has her own business with her daughter. Her hobbies include listening to 80s music (she is a huge *Boy George* and *Culture Club* fan) reading and volunteering at her local stables.

I dedicate this book to myself, to my parents, my daughter, my husband and my family who have helped and supported me.

Angela Newland

I AM MUM

AUSTIN MACAULEY PUBLISHERS™
LONDON • CAMBRIDGE • NEW YORK • SHARJAH

Copyright © Angela Newland 2022

The right of Angela Newland to be identified as author of this work has been asserted by the author in accordance with sections 77 and 78 of the Copyright, Designs and Patents Act 1988.

All rights reserved. No part of this publication may be reproduced, stored in a retrieval system, or transmitted in any form or by any means, electronic, mechanical, photocopying, recording, or otherwise, without the prior permission of the publishers.

Any person who commits any unauthorised act in relation to this publication may be liable to criminal prosecution and civil claims for damages.

A CIP catalogue record for this title is available from the British Library.

ISBN 9781398481077 (Paperback)
ISBN 9781398481084 (ePub e-book)

www.austinmacauley.com

First Published 2022
Austin Macauley Publishers Ltd®
1 Canada Square
Canary Wharf
London
E14 5AA

Thanks to all those involved in getting my book to publication.

To my daughter who helped me and listened to my ramblings, to my husband who encouraged me to go for it and to Austin Macauley Publishers and their team for bringing it all together and making it all a possibility for me.

I Am Mum

I am a mum and a step-mum. These are two very different experiences of being a mum for me—so many challenges and obstacles every day, the highs and the lows, the good and the bad. I wanted to write this book to reach out to other mums, step-mums and stepparents and share my heartfelt experience and my reality, to explain how in comparison my experience of being a biological mum is to being a step-mum. It highlights more of the side of things that nobody would admit to or talk about—the harder side, the not-so-nice side, but I feel that this should be talked about and shared as I would hate to think that there is someone out there thinking that what they are doing is not enough, or that their struggle is not real, or that they are doing something wrong. Our parenting situations are unique, and I hope that from mine someone will learn something valuable about how unique and precious their individual situation is, and how they are not alone in their struggles. All the things that I have experienced have made me truly look at myself as a parent and look at my stepchildren and what they have been through. It has been a real rollercoaster ride so far, and I'm hopeful that me talking about this will encourage others to not be ashamed to speak about how they have felt as a parent and stepparent, and to not feel like I have… that nobody understands or wants to listen or help. I cannot stress enough how important this is for your mental health and wellbeing. I have thought seriously about starting up some sort of charity or support group for stepparents, specifically who are not having the whole my-step-kids-are-amazing experience, who have had to face challenges alone, where there has been no help available and all they really needed was someone to listen, empathise, understand and not judge.

The dynamics of a blended family are complex at the best of times, and there are reasons this has been so difficult for me. I am an only child. My daughter is an only child, and we were a unit. We then inherited for me a new partner, and for my daughter three step siblings. It is not always a case of the blending being trouble-free and amazing. I imagine when the children involved are babies or toddler-age, it is slightly easier, but when they are older and near teens, it can be incredibly difficult for all involved. Whether it is hormones, clashes of personalities, jealousy, resentment, anger or all of the above, it is so hard on all involved. The transition and change are unsettling for the kids, and the parents/stepparents are on edge, as situations arise where there are differences in rules, upbringing, opinions and how they are disciplined; the list goes on. It helps massively if the ex-partners involved are cooperative with co-parenting, but in our situation, neither mine nor Blake's ex-partners were on board with it. They just wanted to fight it out at every opportunity. This just made things harder than was necessary.

There are so many elements of this journey that could have been so different. I feel if the exes had been more focused on parenting than being at war with us, the focus would always have been the kids, but for them it was not, and this has led the kids to feel in the middle and involved in a war of taking sides. It makes me so angry that they have been so wrapped up in their own selfishness that they have not seen the effects this has had on the kids and their relationship with their kids. I honestly believe they were too selfish to be parents, and I personally take some of the blame for that with my ex, as I chose him! I really think that couples should be able to put their own feelings aside and think more about the children and come up with a way to co-parent to make things better for them.

Anyway, let me make a start and tell you about me and Sienna.

A bit about me and Sienna...

My daughter Sienna was born at 3:26 a.m. on the 1st of September 1996, weighing seven lb one oz—my miracle baby girl. Why do you call her your miracle baby, you ask? Because I found out at age 23 that I had endometriosis. It had taken five years to get a diagnosis and, of course, had implications to my fertility. My doctor said I was being faced with having to make the difficult decision as to whether to try for a baby, or risk leaving it and not ever being able to have any children, and I was devastated. This was a massive thing for me and Sienna's dad, and it put a strain on our relationship because I think he felt like he was too young to be having kids, and that I was trying to somehow trap him. After tears, talking and lots of debating, we decided that we did not want to risk leaving it and not being able to have kids. I was lucky enough to fall pregnant and have my miracle baby girl when I was age 24, one month before my 25th birthday. She was a good baby, toddler and child. Her teens were challenging, but we got through, and I was lucky enough to spend time from when she was born to when she started school at home, enabling me to be there for all the milestones and memories that are now so precious and for which I am so grateful. There were no more babies for me after Sienna, as after difficult 15 years of living with endometriosis and having every treatment and procedure known to man, I had a full hysterectomy at the age of 30. They clarified at that point that if I had decided to leave it and not have children, I would not have been lucky enough to have any due to the mass, that they removed, having pushed up against my womb. So, I knew that we had made the right decision, and I was so conscious of how lucky I was to be able to become a mum and I will always be forever grateful for that privilege, as so many others do not ever get that chance.

At the age of 38, after 16 years of being with Sienna's dad, we split up. It was my decision and not one that I took lightly, as we had got to this point three times over the 16-year period that we had been living together. I should have realised earlier that he did not want to commit or marry and was not going to change, but each time I gave him the benefit of the doubt, hoping that things might change, but they didn't. I started to suspect that things were not going to be any better when we reached the ten-year point in our relationship. I was living the life of a single mum, doing everything on my own, living with someone who had a better relationship with their PlayStation than with me and Sienna, and one day, I just thought this is not how I want my daughter to think relationships should be, and when she grows up and moves out, what will I have? Nothing, just an empty life with a man who does not want to be with me or be a part of this family. It was a really tough time, as Sienna's dad didn't take well to the split. He turned out to be spiteful in that he wanted us out of the house we jointly owned. I asked to keep living there and pay the mortgage until she came out of fulltime education but he said no. I was also trying to deal with all the hurt and emotions Sienna was experiencing with her begging me at one point to take her dad back and give him another chance. I had to say I'm so sorry but I can't, but I knew it was the right thing to do and that she would understand when she was older. And she does! The whole experience was so hard, and when I look back, I realise what strength I had to find to get myself through it and stand by my decision.

After only a few months, I met my husband, Blake. I hadn't intended to get into a relationship at all. I was adamant. I just wanted to be on my own and build a life for me and Sienna. I didn't want to be one of those mums that brings a different guy home each month and ruins their child's life with no routine or stability. She was going through enough, so I knew that when and if I ever met anyone else, I would have to be 100% sure that I wanted to be with him. I was introduced to Blake through a friend, and at the time, we had very similar situations and were going through a lot of the same stuff. It was arranged that he would come to the pub whilst me and my friend were there for a drink. I had told my friend, "He has glasses. I don't like men in glasses!" and said, "Hmm, I'm not sure." My friend persuaded me to talk to him via text, which we did for quite a few weeks and then he asked me on a date. I knew quite early on that I wanted to be with him, and that it would be complicated, but here we are! Blake has three children, Tyler, Theo, and Olivia, and when we met, Sienna was 11, Tyler was 11, Theo was six and Olivia was two-and-a-half. It was strange for Sienna going from being an only child to this blended family, and likewise, Blake's kids were a unit and used to being together, and here was this girl and her mum trying to be a part of their family.

My daughter was by no means happy with me and her dad splitting up, and she will freely admit that she gave my husband a really hard time for a quite few years, but she has a good relationship with Blake now and can turn to him for help and support more than she can with her own dad. I am disappointed with how her dad dealt with things when we split up. Out of spite, he wanted us to move out of the family home that we jointly owned and sell it, which was meant to be Sienna's inheritance. He stopped paying for the internet, so I had to get a temporary fix until we moved out, as Sienna couldn't do her homework. He refused to pay his half of the mortgage because he wasn't living there anymore, so I had to plead with the mortgage company to reduce the payments so that I could afford them myself. He left me to finish getting certificates and minor repairs done and to manage all appointments of any viewings as well as cut the grass and attend to the garden, etc. He wanted nothing to do with any of it, so I also packed down the house and sorted all the contents and what was his, I packed and put back in the loft for him to arrange someone to collect on his behalf. The thing that annoyed me the most was that he was more worried about trying to find a way for me to take him back when I had made it very clear that this was never an option, and for me, he should have been using that time to start from scratch building a relationship with Sienna. I asked him to just make sure that whatever happened, he made Sienna his focus and to concentrate on building a relationship with her, as it was like a second chance, a chance to get it right with her, and he could not even do that. He has played the blame game constantly for years since the split and even blamed Sienna at one point for our split, which in my mind is unforgivable, coming from someone who cannot face his part in it all. He met someone else just as he was beginning to start chipping through the ice with Sienna and then made the mistake of putting them first. As a result, he has not got a good relationship with Sienna now; when they speak, or on the odd occasion meet, there is digging and arguing back and forth because he won't accept that he hasn't been there for her and that he has made mistakes. Sienna is 24 now and engaged to be married herself. I will have the pleasure and honour of walking her down the aisle. If you were to ask her who has always been there for her, I know with my hand on my heart, she would say, "My mum has," and that to me is what being a parent is all about. You don't parent when it suits you; you are a part of that child's life 24/7 even if it's just a text saying, *Are you okay?* when they no longer live at home. You are still responsible for them whether they are babies or adults, and you never stop being their parent. Sadly, not all parents have my sentiment, I know. And her dad does not have that sentiment, he does not know what she is doing in her life, speaks to her once every one – three months, and if you were to ask him why, he would blame me. He would say, "Her mum has made it difficult for me to have a relationship with Sienna."

I say, "No, you did that yourself. Just because it is not easy, you do not give up."

Being a step-mum is not for the fainthearted; you must have strong armour to not let certain things hurt your feelings and to try not to take it all too personally. You find yourself thinking, 'My daughter would never do that,' 'My daughter would never say that,' but do you know what? You have to come to terms with it very early that your step-kids have been raised differently. You didn't birth them, you haven't been their primary carer since birth and as such they don't know your 'ways' as a mum. They haven't had to adhere to your rules, or your way of being a mum or how you love and care for them, and they fight it. They do not appreciate what you do, and they take it all for granted. I know all kids do that to a degree, but it just seems so much worse when you are the stepparent and on the receiving end of it. That is going to sound horrible to some, I know, but it is true.

Step-mums literally do not get any credit in the grand scheme of things. We are a mum but with none of the credit and all of the blame. The harsh reality is that it is not always: "We get on so well, and although I'm not her biological mum, we have such a good bond that people think she is my biological daughter." In fact, it can be so far from that; we spend most our stepparenting picking up where the absent parent has left off and clearing up the mess they do not wish to deal with. We have to deal with their biological mum telling them not to listen to us as we are not their mum. We have all the same responsibilities but none of the parental rights, having to work so hard at making the right decisions for them whilst being constantly fought against, always knowing that it is not you they want it is their mum and that they are okay with you, but you are not their mum, and of course they do think that let us all be honest here. We totally get the "I don't have to listen to you," or "I don't have to do what you say because you're not my mum," all while having the biological parent (in our case) trying to parent from their sofa in another household when they play no part in that child's actual care.

It has honestly felt like I have had two lives running alongside each other, two opposite examples of motherhood. One is where I am both my daughter's mum and dad, her supporter, her adviser and loving mum and enjoying all the highs and the lows of being in her life. Raising her has been relatively easy in comparison to raising my stepchildren. We are remarkably close and have a strong bond. We always have had. Then, there is the other life I have running alongside this one where I am a step-mum, and with that come three stepchildren, a vastly different experience altogether and a very tough job.

I will start by telling you about Tyler...

Tyler

Tyler was 11 and living with his mum when I met Blake. He is the eldest of Blake's three children and was considering moving in with Blake when I met him. He didn't move in with his dad at that point, as his mum had said she would be upset and didn't know what she would do without him, but later down the line, he moved in with us as his mum kicked him out on more than one occasion. She had him labelled as having ADHD and he was on the drug Ritalin; he was like a zombie and was asking us to not make him take the medication that she had been sending with him. My husband ended up taking him to a London hospital and speaking to a specialist doctor that proved Tyler did not have ADHD and should not have been on the Ritalin. I fear this whole scenario was more about Tyler's mum having an excuse for his behaviour and having that control over him. She had freely admitted on more than one occasion that she could not cope with him or his brother. Tyler came to live with us fulltime, and we got him off the Ritalin, but he did not like our rules. He did not like being at school. He rebelled against it to the point of not doing his work in class, not doing his homework, not even going to school sometimes when he was supposed to. He would not go to detentions to the point that I would have to wait until he came home and put him in the car, drive him back to school and sit in the car and wait for him to finish the detention and then bring him home afterwards. He never came home when he was supposed to, so we would have to try and find him. He stole from us. He lied to us, and eventually went to live back with his mum temporarily. He left us a note on his bed, saying,

"I am going to live back with Mum because I am causing too much trouble living here."

I think he was just angry at both of his parents for splitting up and did not at that point really want to live with either of them. He moved out into a house share with my daughter for a brief period, but unfortunately lost his job, and spent the money he received from the government that was meant to be for rent on cigarettes and drink, leaving my daughter to foot all the bills. This ended in them both parting ways, and he went to live with his nan for a short time, and Sienna moved into her own flat. This caused a division between my daughter and Tyler because he took no responsibility for what he had done, never apologised, or tried to pay her back, and to this day does not speak to her and has not ever paid her back. (He owes her over £1000.) At the age of 19, he got his girlfriend pregnant; he had been with her through school on and off, but their relationship was far from stable. He moved in with her and her mother at first, and then to a flat when the baby was born. He, now at the age of 24, has three girls aged five, two and six months. He got married last year, and after six months, he and his wife have now parted ways. He lives between his mum's house and his ex-wife's house and does not see us, or associate with us now—the reason for that I will come back to later.

Theo

Then there is Theo, the middle child. When I met Blake, Theo was six. He was the least troublesome of the three and overshadowed by his siblings being badly behaved a lot of the time. Theo came to live with us when he was seven. We had literally only just got a house together, his mum had asked us to have Theo to give her a break as he and his older brother Tyler were arguing and fighting all the time. Theo basically said to us at the end of the two weeks that he did not want to live with his mum anymore; he wanted to live with us. He went to his mum and told her this and he has been with us ever since; he is now 18. I have looked after him for longer than his biological mother has. Theo has not got a good relationship with his mum and does not visit her or speak to her unless he really must for something. He did okay at school. With average grades and no real behavioural issues, he was a quiet, kind and caring soul, played rugby, loved his computer games and went onto college. Out of my three stepchildren, he has always been the one that has had the most love and respect for me as his stepmother. In his second year of college, he did not cope well with the lockdown due and Covid-19 and decided to drop out. I have felt really hurt and disappointed, as when he was at college, he got to the point that he would go on the bus to college, say he was going, and I believed him, only to be called by the college and told that he hadn't gone in and had clearly met his friends and gone out for the day instead. I made the mistake of thinking that he would not do that to us and that he was not like Tyler and Olivia, but he proved me wrong, for whatever reason which I do not think is a reflection on how we have supported him. I feel it is more about how he feels about himself and life right now. Another thing that has happened since the pandemic is that Theo has grown his hair, started to wear nail varnish and neutral makeup, on two or three occasions came home from parties in a skirt with tights and now goes out just with his friends dressed this way. He does not dress like this at home or when he goes out with us. A few years back, he had told us that he thought he was bisexual. He is clearly unsure of who he is or wants to be and what it is that he really wants out of life. All I know is that he is also suffering in his life because he has issues with his mum, and how she has acted like he does not exist anymore since he decided to live with us. Until he is ready to address those problems and do something about it for himself, then there is not a lot more that I can do as his step-mum at this stage until he is ready to help himself. We just want him to be happy; that is all any parent wants for their kids. He does not want to get a job and has become unhelpful and non-communicative to the point that we only see him for meals pretty much. We have tried to talk to him, offer help and reason with him, but he is not receptive to any of it. It does not help that Theo and Olivia as siblings do not get on well; they clash. Theo thinks Olivia is a pain, dumb and causes trouble, and Olivia thinks Theo is a goodie-two-shoes, the family favourite, clever and cannot really relate to him much. I have tried with both kids to get them to have family film nights and get involved at home and visiting relatives and days out, but they are at the age where they just want their own space a lot of the time. Theo is 18 and is keeping us at a distance for now. Part of me wonders if this is all because of what has happened to Olivia and her coming to live with us, and the part his mum has played in it all, but I will explain more about that later. Recently, Theo quite angrily told me and my husband that by asking him what he is doing with his life and what jobs he is looking for, or if he intends to go back to college, the way we talk to him, makes him feel like he and his life are a failure. This makes me very sad and somewhat disappointed that after doing our best to support his decision to drop out of college and for at least six months to not do anything at all, I feel that he just wanted someone to blame for the fact that he knows he hasn't made any smart choices for himself. His childlike "I'm not doing that because that's what they want me to do" has backfired on him and he is looking for someone to blame. We have recently found out that Theo is transgender and identifies as Aiyla. This all came out only because Olivia's friend said that her sister knew Theo but not as Theo because Theo is trans and called Aiyla. I asked Theo about this, and he said this was true. I said, "Why could you not tell us this? Why have we had to hear it from a stranger?"

He said, "Because I didn't feel comfortable because of Dad." There was an angry exchange after this, as when Theo had first come home after a drunken night out in a skirt, my husband assumed he had been dressed like that by his mates as a prank and in a joke. (And it was a joke, as my husband is not homophobic, sexist, racist or discriminative in any way.)

He said to Theo whilst laughing, "Oh my God, go and take that off, you poof." Well, Theo had clearly taken offence to this, so I said to him, "If this has offended you, surely it would have made sense to say at this point, 'Dad, I know that you are joking, but I find it offensive because I am actually transgender,' rather than expect us to support and understand when we are kept in the dark and don't know about you wanting to be identified as transgender." We have both clearly told him we love him and will support whoever he wants to be, and it makes no difference to us, but he is carrying this anger for his dad right now. I also wanted to say to him, "If you did not feel you could tell your dad, why couldn't you confide in me?" So, we are now trying to find a way forward from this that we can all adjust, adapt, understand and support each other. It has been another blow that we feel we have shouldered the blame for not understanding something we knew nothing about, and I fear, as a result, are faced with a lot of tough changes for all of us. It just upsets me that he did not feel he could tell us, and part of me thinks of it as quite disrespectful as well to live under the same roof as us with no explanation as to what is wrong, why he is unhappy and has just let us keep worrying and wondering why he has been the way he has at home. Maybe I just feel offended, as I have always thought that Theo could or would speak to me if he had a problem or needed help or advice. I think it is more for me about the reminder that yet again I am left feeling as if I have failed as a step-mum. I guess I need to not take things so personally to a degree, but then as a mum/parent/carer, do you not always strive to make sure that you do your best for your children? And although I know I always try my best, it doesn't mean that they think I have done my best, does it?

My husband literally feels like his kids blame him for everything, and, I have to say as an outsider looking in it, does seem by their behaviour and how they speak to him that they do blame him. It's like they blame him for the split between him and their mum, even though it was their mum that instigated it; he didn't have a clue it was coming, didn't want to split up and did everything he could to make it as easy on the kids as is possible in a breakup situation. When I met him, his ex-wife was actually taking full advantage of that to her own good, to the point that I said, "I think you need to set some boundaries for her," as she was asking him to have the kids most of the time. It was like she didn't want them anymore either, which I said was unfair on him. He had moved out of the family home and was living in a one-bedroom apartment and she was totally pushing for everything to be her way or no way. To be fair, when I look back, that's what she has been like ever since. It's that old chestnut that she does not want to be with him but wants him to still do everything he did before and does not want anyone else to have him because then he will not be there for her as a cash point, babysitter and general problem solver. I think that they should have all had some kind of family counselling for them all to have a better relationship going forwards, eliminate some of the resentment to each other and their situation, and it would also have helped with Blake and his ex with co-parenting arrangements going forwards, as there has been none. I guess some would say it is easy to see this in hindsight, and some would say it's never too late, but none of them would agree to do this now.

One thing I cannot stand about stepparenting is the blame game. I get blamed for so much more than the biological parents because it is easier for them to do that. Although it is expected to a degree, it is still hurtful and not something I feel I deserved. You hear horror stories of stepparents being horrible, evil, nasty and not wanting to have anything to do with their step-kids, but then there are some of us who are the complete opposite to that, who have just tried to bring up their step-kids as they would their own kids and given them the love, care and support they need as best they can. That is what makes it so much harder when they do not acknowledge or appreciate that you are doing your best. I never ever imagined when I first met my husband how hard it would be. There will always be the clashes because you are not their parent, goes with the territory, and the normal stuff of them in the early days not accepting that their parents aren't getting back together any time soon, trying to adapt to the different houses, weekend visits and complete change in their life through no fault of their own. I totally understand how hard that must have been, but we are now talking 11 years down the line, so part of me is not as sympathetic because they are not kids now; they are teens. They want to be treated as adults but don't want to act like one. Surely, there has to come a time when they have to be responsible for how they treat another human being and make them feel? It's not just me this will affect, is it? As they will not be able to treat others like this—teachers, bosses and partners will not want to be treated in such a way that they are blamed, feel unloved and unappreciated, disrespected, used and not needed, whilst my step-kids will see no fault on their side with their behaviour. I cannot stress enough that in my opinion—which may not count for much I know—kids should be taught at an early age to be responsible for themselves, how they act towards others, how they speak to others, to use their manners and to basically be honest, true and try their best—all very basic but so very important in life, and although you may be thinking that it won't get you a long way in life, it will at least make you a half decent person. You can have all the qualifications in the world, but they mean nothing if you are a rude, ignorant or a selfish liar who does not want to help or take responsibility for anything in life. It does make me wonder what society is teaching our kids.

Olivia

Olivia was only two-and-a-half when I met Blake, the youngest of his three kids. She did not understand that her mum and dad had split up and would not be getting back together. All I remember is how upset she would get when she had to leave him and go back to her mum. She was a real daddy's girl and would not leave his side. Olivia has always been spoilt by her mum, not with her love and time, just by giving in to what Olivia wants, which has been a real thorn in my side. Olivia could not decide who she wanted to live with; she likes being at both Mum's and Dad's. This would result in her literally refusing to get in or out of the car when she was being collected or taken back to and from her mum's. So, in the end, when she was eight, Blake had to go to court about custody. It was after a lot of time and money that it was decided by the court that what was best for Olivia was to stay with her mum for one week and then with her dad for one week; she was happy with this because she got to see them both and did not feel like she was having to choose.

What Happened

Things took a traumatic turn when at the age of 12 years old, Olivia reported to her school that her mum's boyfriend (Marcus) was touching her. We only found this out when a police officer and social services turned up at the door with her, as it was her week with us. A statement was taken, and social services wrote their report. The outcome was that Marcus was not charged by the police, as it was Olivia's word against his and there was no physical evidence; social services, however, told us that Marcus had been touching Olivia inappropriately and grooming her and that she would only be deemed safe if she were to come and live with us fulltime, and so she did. Olivia wanted to live with her mum, but her mum was not prepared to get her boyfriend to leave, and she told Olivia she did not believe her, and if she had evidence that Marcus has done these things to her, then she would ask him to leave, but she has not, so she cannot ask him to. Olivia accepted this. I thought it was appalling personally as a parent to choose a man over her child, but that is my opinion. Most of Olivia's mum's side of the family turned against Olivia at this point, including her older brother, Tyler, who decided to believe their mum's side of the story.

What We Have Done

We were in no way prepared for how this was going to be. What it is like dealing with a girl who has been a victim of sexual trauma, I struggle to put into words. We firstly went on the waiting list for Olivia to receive counselling from CARA (Centre of Action on Rape and Abuse). She was given only six sessions of counselling, but she had refused to speak about what had happened. They advised us that this was common and that it may be years before she felt she could talk about what had happened. Olivia's behaviour rapidly declined from this point. She started self-harm, smoking, both normal cigarettes and pot. She was taking my things and stealing from a local store and lying to us, but the one thing we could not have been prepared for was the nude pictures; she started to send nude pictures of herself to boys. She didn't even see what the problem was with it; she saw it as normal, and she didn't just do it once. She did it on at least six occasions. On one occasion, she had pictures taken from her phone where a so-called 'friend' at the time fell out with her and she had stupidly shared her passwords with this girl, who then went on to give them to a girl Olivia did not have a good relationship with, who then gave them to a boy in school a year above Olivia, who leaked them to everyone. This incident ended up with the police investigating it, as Olivia was not the only girl that he had done this to, and he was doing other things too. It was whilst this investigation was going on that she went and sent a 'nude' photograph to a boy. I told the police this, as I could not believe that being involved in an investigation did not make her realise how serious this was, or how dangerous. I had tried to get help from the school. I had tried to refer her back to EMHWS (Emotional Mental Health and Wellbeing Services), but their take was that unless she has already got arrested or hurt herself, they cannot help me. I spoke to CARA, as they had given me some support on understanding behaviours of someone who has been a victim of sexual trauma, but I seemed to be getting sent around in a circle and I was told to look on websites for advice and support, which was no help. What nobody realises is every single day is a battle; she would argue, fight, refuse to do things, ask for things and, when told 'no', would have the equivalence of a five-year-old's tantrum, throwing herself on the floor, kicking and wailing. She wouldn't go to sleep, wouldn't get up, would steal food from the cupboards and then not eat her dinner. She started smoking, was lying about where she was and who she was with, would find a way to get her own way whatever it took, was talking in a very sexual way, very dirty-minded and potty-mouthed, was swearing, had no respect for herself or anyone else and freely admitted being bad was more fun; she was literally off the rails. It felt like the more we tried to help her, the more set she was on turning the other way and running from it.

Tyler's Wedding

This brings me back to Tyler briefly; Tyler announced he was getting married. He wanted us all to go to his wedding, even though he had also invited Marcus. My husband had said to Tyler that he couldn't go with Marcus there, as he could not stand in a room with a man who had done this to his daughter and not react; it was too much. Heartbreakingly, Tyler decided to take the advice of his mum and his fiancé and his fiancé's mum and disinvited myself and Blake for this reason. They could see no problem with what was being asked of my husband and, instead, blamed him for making Tyler choose and for spoiling their special day. Olivia and Theo were still invited and wanted to attend, so I had to check with social services this would be okay, as Marcus would be there. They agreed it would be okay if Olivia had a chaperone, so Blake's mum took them to the wedding. To this day, Tyler is still not speaking to Blake, and we do not see our three grandchildren anymore because of all of this. All we were doing was what we thought was right by protecting Olivia and refusing to be in the same room as Olivia's perpetrator (which I think was a big question for my husband: how many men could be in the same room as the man that has been touching their daughter inappropriately and grooming her?). This is all because Tyler thinks Olivia has lied, as does her mum, as she has no proof of what happened and that it was her word against Marcus, and there have been no charges against him by the police. This is even after in the report from social services; it clearly states that Olivia's mum willingly told them that this is not the first time something has happened between Olivia and Marcus, and that how she dealt with it last time was by making sure Olivia was not left alone with Marcus at all, and she cannot see the problem with it. Does this sound to you like a woman who can be trusted to make the right decisions to keep her child safe? I will leave that for you to ponder. Tyler has a lot of anger towards Blake, and it makes me really sad that all we have done is loved, cared for and supported him throughout and he has taken the side of his mum and excluded his dad from his life. That's basically what has happened. We don't know how we are going to be able to come back from this. Maybe it will just take time.

What Now

We do our best to protect Olivia and support her through what has been such a hard time for her and such a traumatic thing for her to deal with. I don't know if it will get any easier, but I have managed to get Olivia some help from the children's society in the form of what they call a care course, which is fully funded and the school applied for on her behalf. She learns about child and sexual exploitation, online safety, consent, permission, sexual health and lots of other things. I have also been referred for parental support from Barnardo's, which is amazing. All I have asked for throughout all this is for there to be someone to ask the questions and just let me talk about it, things like: 'Am I doing okay? Is this really what's best for Olivia? I'm finding this hard. Who can I talk to? Does anyone even understand or care? What should I do?' Sometimes, it is just a lot to carry, and I was shocked at the system and how there is no help out there until something really serious happens because it should never get to that, and it has made me seriously think about the support available to parents just to be able to talk about their own unique situations and how we don't fit into a box. We can't be dealt with by following a script, and we are often pushed aside because we don't fit criteria for help. I honestly feel like I need respite from this situation, and there is none. I can accept that now because I have someone, I know is there from Barnardo's when nobody else is. Friends can be judgemental because they don't understand your situation and quite openly say they wouldn't want to be in your situation, which is hurtful sometimes, as we are still a family unit and nobody is perfect after all. Relatives get cross because of the amount of stress and pressure we face and worry for our health and wellbeing; it isn't until you sit and explain to someone what's been going on in your week that you realise the enormity of what you are dealing with and how you normalise it as your everyday life. We are still a family and have a life to lead, and we have other kids to consider—a house, bills, jobs, dogs, appointments, parents and responsibilities, and we are trying to fit all of that around what feels like this explosive bomb ticking away in the middle of it all. I would say to other stepparents to always talk to someone. There is no shame in finding it hard. Always fight for help, support and advice because it could make all the difference to you, your family, your situation and how you can deal with it. I have personally found that you get a bit lost in it all; it is so overwhelming and there is so much to try and sort out with Olivia that it can literally take over my life. I have had to make a conscious effort to step back and evaluate what I can do for myself because I feel like I have lost myself in it all. My own needs and life have taken a backseat in the grand scheme of things, and I have carried a lot of responsibility, difficult decision making and propping up the family in hard times as well as being on the receiving end of Olivia's unhappiness. This is always going to influence you personally and you need to acknowledge that and not be scared to admit it to someone. I've had counselling in the past for when I split up with Sienna's dad, and luckily, the methods I have taken from those sessions have helped me through this—writing things down, times for reflection, communicating, trying to stay healthy and positive and above all, talking about it. I think that is one of the most important pieces of advice I would give to someone; don't feel embarrassed or judged by others. It's not your bad parenting or your child's bad behaviour. You don't need sympathy for how bad your kid is. You just need to find someone who will listen without judgement. This is where I have been so lucky with Barnardo's.

Blake

My husband, Blake—I love this man. He is my soulmate; I wish I had met him sooner, as I am so very conscious that we met late in life, and we have so much to fit in and catch up on together. Obviously, if I had met him sooner, I would not have my daughter, and I would not be without her, but you understand what I mean. He has always been hands-on with his kids, and it is so lovely how he supports them, and how he is as a stepdad to my daughter means so much to me. He is 100%there for her as her stepdad. How all of this has affected him has been heartbreaking to watch. It makes me want to cry just thinking about it now; he has wanted only the best for all his kids, and they do not seem to appreciate that. We have had to stand strong as a team with all that has gone on. Due to the delicate nature of what has happened to Olivia, I have dealt with most things. My husband has found it hard enough to not react to the situation and towards his ex-wife and her partner, by telling himself that it would not help Olivia if he was in prison for reacting to them. The family as a whole has gone through a lot and have weathered the storm. I and my husband have just tried to stay strong together and try our hardest not to let all of these things interfere with our relationship when the kids move on in life. We still want there to be an 'us', and it would be so easy to let their behaviour affect us sometimes, so we work hard at making time for us. I hope that the love and support that I give him, and his kids, has helped him through all this. He watches his children who are all suffering in their own way at the expense of a selfish mother. She instigated their split and divorce, stating that he was not interested in her, or the kids, and that he was always going out and selfish and did not want to be at home. In all honesty, that sounds more like a mirror statement of her behaviour because this is what I have witnessed in the time I have known him and the kids, and she is still the same to this day. We have been together for 11.5 years and married for 10 of those. I am thankful every day for the fact that I met this man and that he is a part of my life. Through all that is difficult, when you scrape it all back, there is still us.

What puzzles me is that his children have not been more receptive to me as their step-mum. I could totally understand it if I was nasty, unfair, had favourites, treated them any differently to my own daughter or made their lives difficult. I didn't want to be around them, didn't help or support them, didn't encourage them to see their mum or tried to come between them and their dad, but I have done none of those things. All I have ever done is try to bring them up in a safe, secure, loving and caring environment with stability and boundaries. I have tried to get to know them, help them, care for them and generally be there for them throughout. I often wonder if the reason they are not receptive to me is because they are resentful that I am who I am. I am too nice and too helpful, and they want to be able to dislike me with good reasons. It sounds childish, but I feel that all their attitudes to their parents' divorcing is still very immature. They blame my husband for the split, whereas it was his ex-wife that instigated the split, and they refuse to accept that and instead act as though he abandoned them, even though it is him. They all live or have lived with. Some aspects of the situation really do baffle me. It also makes me think that the ex-wife has quite clearly tried to turn the kids against their dad at any given opportunity, and I know for a fact she is definitely not my biggest fan, but again, she does not have a reason to be that way when all I have done is bring up her children where she could not, or did not, want to.

The Biological Mum

It says something to me as a parent when all three children have ended up living with their dad, through choice or otherwise. It still is not deemed as normal; generally kids live with their mum. I think that my step-kids' biological mum for one individual has had such a toxic effect on so many lives that it literally makes me want to scream at her, "You don't deserve to be a mum! You didn't deserve my husband, and you don't deserve your kids. You have failed all of them." Don't get me wrong. She has never done anything to me personally. She has always been civil, even if only just, and has in that sense given me no reason to have any bad feeling towards her, but as a mum myself, she stands for everything I despise in a so-called parent. She has first and foremost chosen a man over her own child. She has pushed away all her children at some point. She takes no responsibility for them and lays all the blame at our door. She wants to control how the kids are brought up, even though she is not in any position to do that herself and literally sees them on her terms. Another thing she will not do is co-parent and will not accept that I look after her children and have an element of responsibility for them and have done to date for the 12 years I have known my husband! She refuses to accept I exist, saying she will only speak to my husband about anything relating to the kids, or to them directly. All this tells me is that she sees me as a threat, a threat to the tiny thread of hope she has of her children wanting to be a part of her life, wanting her to be their mum and having any sort of relationship with them going forwards. To me, it is just showing how in all this the one thing she has not given the right priority or consideration to are her children. With this example of a parent and primary carer, it does make me realise that it is no wonder that my stepchildren have suffered as they have. It makes me sad and angry at the same time that my step-kids have not had from their mum what my daughter has had from me, even though I try my hardest to give them that even if they do not seem to want it from me. The harsh realities of how different people can be and what they see their role as a parent being is off the scale and not something I can get my head around. Maybe it is purely the fact that I cherish motherhood and, early on, was so very grateful that I had that opportunity in my life, or maybe it is just the fact that some people are just not cut out to be parents; they are too selfish or were not ready to be a parent. I will leave you to ponder on that one.

I have the ultimate respect for all stepparents. I fully understand what that responsibility and experience is like, and how different it is or can be, and I know that I haven't celebrated with you any of the highs and all of the lows, but in all honesty, this family has had trauma thrown into the mix, so it will be some time before I can celebrate any highs. I just cherish the little things and the small moments where I see the kids happy and smiling because there haven't been that many big things in my journey as a stepparent as yet that I have been able to celebrate with them. I hold onto the hope that later in their life, the kids will all step back and realise that all I and my husband were trying to do was the best by them—from the bottom of our hearts. If you are doing your best by them, then that is enough; your best is always good enough, and always remember that, although you are not their biological parent, you have stepped up and taken on that duty to fill the gap where the other parent decided to step back and not be a part of it. What you are doing is scary, admirable, kind, brave, amazing, selfless, hard, frustrating, challenging, and on occasion rewarding, but do not let anyone make you feel like what you are doing means nothing or is not enough, because it is. They are not in your unique situation, and they do not come up against the things that you do every day, so they will never truly understand the overwhelming enormity of your family situation. Be proud of what you are doing for your stepchildren because without you, they would not have the life they have, and I for one know how important it is for someone to tell you that and to feel that what you are doing matters because you do not hear it enough from them or others.

Quite sadly, I have got to a point where I am not enjoying my experience of being a step-mum, and that is hard to say. I had so hoped that by now, my relationship with all three of Blake's kids would be better, but if anything, it is worse. I know it is not my fault, but that does not mean that it makes it okay either. Every day, I am living in an environment where I feel like I am being lied to, used, disrespected and disliked. It does not stop me from doing what I do, but it has made me question if I should stay, and I resent my situation for that. I should not feel like I should not live in my house with my stepchildren, that I am not welcome in my own home, that I am just there when it suits them. I have spoken to my husband about how I feel, and he understands and supports me, but at the end of the day, I realise these are his children, and I would not want to put him in a position that he feels he has to choose. He has spoken to them about how they have made me feel and that I am considering leaving, and it has made no difference. What does this tell me? It most definitely makes me feel unwanted—that is for sure—and unhappy, sad and hurt; I could go on. I am sure that what I have written here resonates with so many others. It's that ugly truth that nobody talks about but should! We face it together and always find a way through, and it is a good job that we have each other when push comes to shove because parenting is certainly not for the fainthearted. Kids do not come with a manual, and even if they did, each one is very different and very unique. It's a big responsibility and a hard job looking after them, but in our situation, these kids haven't had it easy at all. This is where you get bumps in the road. We cannot all be perfect, and we will be judged (I am all the time as a step-mum!) but I hope that other families will realise that it is not always as it seems, and all we can do is try our best in these situations and listen and learn from each other. Be kind. As a parent, don't ever say, "I'm so glad that's not my child!" because you never know what life situations are going to come along and affect you or your kids and when you might need help, support, advice, a kind word, a listening ear or a shoulder to cry on. Remember: nobody is perfect!

Where this leaves us now is standing at a crucial point in our extremely hard journey together as a family, one which I do not know the outcome of, but all I do know is that throughout it all, as I have said on so many occasions…

I am Mum.

The End